The Story of Snow Leopard

By

James Patrick (Jamie) Baldwin

The contents of this book regarding the accuracy of events, people and places depicted; permissions to use all previously published materials; and opinions expressed; are the sole responsibility of the author, who assumes all liability for the contents of this book and indemnifies the publisher against any claims stemming from the publication of this book.

International Standard Book Number 978-1-09115-469-8

Snow Leopard: *a moderately large cat native to the mountain ranges of Central Asia, mainly in the Pamir Mountains of Tajikistan (photograph by Steve Winter)*

Table of Contents

Preface

I was visiting the new offices of the US Department of Commerce's "Business Information Services for the Newly Independent States" (BISNIS), a small unit within the department that provided guidance and information to companies and individuals wishing to do business with the newly independent former Soviet Republics. During my visit I learned about an airline operation in Tajikistan involving a Boeing 747SP, named *Snow Leopard*, that was operating between London and Dushanbe, the capital, by Tajik Air, the national airline of Tajikistan, and crewed by former pilots, pursers and flight attendants of the former Pan American World Airways (Pan Am). The aircraft itself was also formerly owned by Pan Am. Having been a longtime fan of Pan Am, I jumped at the possibility of getting involved with the operation.

I became Tajik Air's US Representative looking for investment in the operation as well as for expertise to assist the civil aviation sector of Tajikistan. What happened during the operation is narrated in these pages. Needless to say, it could have succeeded. Unfortunately, fate was not on the side of Tajikistan.

Time has gone by since those days of hope and now perhaps fate will change, and the operation envisioned then could become reality one day soon.

James Patrick (Jamie) Baldwin
Cambridge, Maryland

Acknowledgements

Writing this story would not have been possible without the contributions of those Pan Am pilots and flight attendants who were so willing to share their experiences. I would like to personally pay tribute to the late Pan Am Captain Sherman Carr whose narrative about his experiences with *Snow Leopard* played a major part in this story (and the operation) and former Pan Am Pursers Gunilla Crawford, Tania Anderson and Vince Rossi. I would also like to thank Ben Daneshmand with whom I worked in London for his recollections of the events he shared with me.

Photos and images are from the author's collection or courtesy of Gunilla Crawford and Vince Rossi, unless otherwise noted.

Chapter I

The Aircraft and the Operation

The Aircraft

THIS IS THE STORY ABOUT AN AIRCRAFT NAMED *SNOW LEOPARD,* which was a Boeing 747SP that was leased by Tajik Air, the national airline of the Republic of Tajikistan, then a newly independent former Soviet Republic located in Central Asia. The aircraft was operated exclusively on the international routes of Tajik Air and gave that airline a presence in London, UK, Delhi, India and Karachi, Pakistan. The operation was controlled and managed by a management company in London, Tajik Air Limited. This is what made this operation unique. What also made it unique was that *Snow Leopard* was crewed by former pilots and flight attendants of Pan American World Airways (Pan Am), the former great airline that ceased operations in December 1991.

The operation started with *Snow Leopard's* departure from London for Dushanbe, Tajikistan in December 1993. It ended in February 1994 when the aircraft was repossessed by United Airlines, the aircraft's owner and lessor. What happened during these three months are stories of adventure, bravery, comedy, intrigue, loyalty, and teamwork. And they will be told here by those who were there, the pilots, flight attendants and the London management staff.

As background, the Boeing 747SP is a modified version of the Boeing 747, which was designed for ultra-long-range flights. The "SP" stands for "Special Performance". Compared with its predecessor, the 747-100, the 747SP retained its wide-body four-engine layout, along with its double-deck design, but had a shortened fuselage, larger vertical stabilizer, and simplified trailing edge flaps. The weight saved by the shortened fuselage permitted longer range and increased speed relative to other 747 configurations.

Known during development as the short-body 747SB, the 747SP was designed to meet a 1973 joint request from Pan Am and Iran Air, who were looking for a high-capacity airliner with sufficient range to cover Pan Am's New York–Middle Eastern routes and Iran Air's planned Tehran–New York route. The aircraft also was intended to provide Boeing with a mid-size wide-body airliner to compete with the DC-10 and L-1011.

The 747SP first entered service with Pan Am in 1976. The aircraft was later acquired by VIP and government customers, but sales did not meet the expected 200 units, and production ultimately totaled 45 aircraft.

While in service, the 747SP set several aeronautical performance records, including three record-setting round-the-world flights, two operated by Pan Am and the third by United.

Captain Sherman Carr, one of the former Pan Am pilots who flew *Snow Leopard*:

> *"The airplane that was to be used for this operation was a Boeing 747SP. The plane was originally developed for Pan Am to be able to operate non-stop from the U.S. to Hong Kong and be able to stay aloft for over 15 hours. It was actually a regular 747 with upstairs lounge seating but shortened by about 48 feet to make it lighter and additional fuel tanks for longer range. If it's not loaded with full fuel for extended range flights, the aircraft actually scoots like a hot rod and will outperform any WWII or Korean conflict fighter aircraft and is a lot of fun to fly. It will roll or loop or do most of the maneuvers you see at airshows but of course this is not authorized so no pilot would ever tell you he had done those things. For Dushanbe, surrounded by mountains in all directions, it was the perfect choice due to its ability to climb quickly, safely and be on its way in a timely manner and still carry about 260 people with an extended first class."*

Snow Leopard, Manufacturer's Serial Number 21649, Serial 373 was first delivered to Pan American World Airways on 11 May 1979 registered as N540PA and named *Clipper White Falcon*. It was renamed *Clipper Flying Arrow* on 1 August 1979 and later renamed *Clipper Star of the Union* on 1 January 1980. One year later, on 1 January 1981, the aircraft became *China Clipper*.

On 12 February 1986, as part of Pan Am's sale of its Pacific Routes, N540PA was acquired by United Airlines. The registration was changed to N149UA on 1 June 1986. It was under this registration that the aircraft operated for Tajik Air, pictured below:

After the aircraft was repossessed by United Airlines, it was bought by the Brunei Government and re-registered as V8-JBB. It was then bought by the Government of Bahrain on 24 December 1998 and registered as A9C-HMH (below).

Snow Leopard's most recent owner was Las Vegas Sands Corporation, registered as VQ-BMS (below, photo by Wong Chi Lam). Unfortunately, while parked in a hangar at Lake Charles-Chennault International Airport, Louisiana, USA, Hurricane Laura struck on 27 August 2020.

The doors of the hangar were blown out by strong winds and the aircraft sustained serious damage. The right-hand wing tip of the aircraft struck a steal beam of the hangar structure, causing the tip to separate. The wing of another aircraft impacted the lower nose section of the aircraft, causing a massive tear (photo of damaged aircraft via the Flight Safety Foundation).

Starting a new service in any market requires a great deal of research and planning. There must be a suitable aircraft. Government approvals must be in place. Airport access, slots (if required), ground handling services and airport facilities (check-in desks, etc.) must be obtained. On the commercial side, the new service needs to be marketed, publicized and tickets sold. Other details include setting up the ticket and operations offices, arranging catering, publishing an In-Flight magazine, and printing safety information cards, timetables, paper tickets, baggage tickets, promotional materials and stationery.

For Tajik Air, however, there was one very important requirement missing: an operating base in London and sufficient infrastructure to crew and maintain a Boeing 747SP aircraft. That presented a huge problem as the civil aviation structure of Tajikistan was completely inexperienced in intercontinental operations. In fact, Tajik Air was created by the breaking-up of the Soviet Union and the then national carrier Aeroflot's leaving of some old Russian-built aircraft (mostly TU-154s) for use by Tajik Air as the new national air carrier of Tajikistan. Setting up a London base would seem impossible to achieve given the limited resources of Tajikistan. However, through the foresight and creativeness of a few airline experts in London, the requirement was met.

To establish the necessary infrastructure so that Tajik Air could operate flights to/from London, a third-party UK management company, Tajik Air Limited, was formed. Its purpose was to operate international flights on behalf of Tajik Air. The company would obtain and maintain the aircraft and crew, organize the marketing and sales of tickets and operate the flights. This would be accomplished using Tajikistan's Air Operator's Certificate (AOC) and Tajik Air's call-sign and airline code. Tajikistan committed to funding the new service and also obtaining the required government permissions for the operation.

How would this operation be viable and profitable? The route of primary interest to Tajik Air was the London (Heathrow) (LHR)-Dushanbe (DYU) sector. Operating that sector as an Origin-Destination route presented problems in that there was little, if any, traffic between the two points. The question was how to fill an aircraft with 260 seats? The answer: Offer service between LHR and points beyond DYU. This was to be accomplished using rights under the Sixth Freedom of the Air.

The Freedoms of the Air, established by the Chicago Convention of 1944, are a set of commercial aviation rights granting a country's airlines the privilege of entering and landing in another country's airspace. The table below illustrates these Freedoms of the Air:

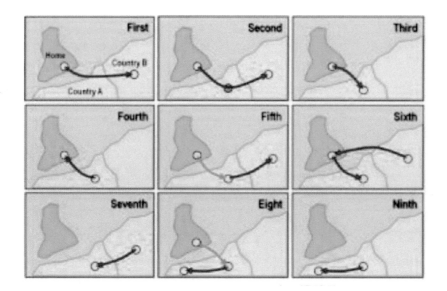

In the case of Tajik Air, the Third and Fourth Freedoms were the operative. The former gives the "Home" (Tajikistan) country the rights to carry commercial traffic (passengers/cargo/mail, etc.) to another country; the latter gives the "Home" country the rights to carry commercial traffic from that other country to home. These rights are generally agreed-to between the "Home" country and the other country in the form of a Bilateral Agreement or an Air Services Agreement. By using Third and Fourth Freedom rights, a Sixth Freedom operation can be created. It is similar to a hub operation with the home country being in the middle of the operation between two different countries.

For Tajik Air, the beyond points selected were Delhi, India (DEL) and Karachi, Pakistan (KHI) due to the large number of Indians and Pakistanis living in the UK. The schedule would work like this: Tajik Air departs from LHR with a planeload of passengers on a Fourth Freedom flight to DYU. Upon arrival in DYU, those few passengers destined for DYU disembark and the rest stay on board. The flight then departs DYU with a new flight number on a Third Freedom flight for DEL or KHI. Upon turning around in DEL/KHI, with a new planeload of passengers, the flight becomes a Fourth Freedom to DYU and from DYU, with another flight number, Third Freedom to LHR. By operating this schedule, Tajik Air could fill the seats of *Snow Leopard*, and compete in a highly competitive market by offering good service with low fares. To operate this schedule, Bilateral or Air Services agreements were required for scheduled traffic between Tajikistan and India/Pakistan in addition to the UK.

The published timetable shown below illustrates this operation. Baggage tags are also shown.

TAJIK AIR

THE AIRLINE OF
THE REPUBLIC OF TAJIKISTAN

Tajik Air, the airline of
the Republic of
Tajikistan, operates
scheduled flights world-
wide. Its combination
of modern aircraft,
passenger comfort,
warm hospitality,
excellent catering and
outstanding in-flight
services, makes Tajik
Air the ideal choice for
business and leisure
travellers alike.

Delhi
Dushanbe
Karachi
Khujand
London
Moscow
Sharjah
St. Petersburg
Yerevan

Tajik Air
98 Macmillan House
Kensington High Street
London W8 4SG
Tel. 071 897 7788

Flights are subject to government approval and change without prior notice.

TIMETABLE
UNITED KINGDOM
WINTER 1993/1994

TAJIK AIR

QUICK REFERENCE GUIDE
FLIGHTS TO/FROM LONDON HEATHROW

DEPARTURES

ROUTE	DAY	DEP	ARR	VIA	FLIGHT NOS	AIRCRAFT
London (LHR) - Delhi (DEL)	Mon	2215	1315*	Dushanbe	7J800 / 7J827	747SP
	Thu	2215	1315*	Dushanbe	7J801 / 7J820	747SP
	Sun	1130	1230*	Dushanbe	7J806 / 7J825	747SP
London (LHR) - Dushanbe (DYU)	Mon	2215	0645*		7J806	747SP
	Thu	2215	0645*		7J801	747SP
	Fri	2215	0645*		7J807	747SP
	Sun	2130	0600*		7J809	747SP
London (LHR) - Karachi (KHI)	Fri	2215	1300*	Dushanbe	7J807 / 7J830	747SP
London (LHR) - Yerevan (EVN)	Sat	2215	0645*	Dushanbe	7J811	747SP

ARRIVALS

ROUTE	DAY	DEP	ARR	VIA	FLIGHT NOS	AIRCRAFT
Delhi (DEL) - London (LHR)	Mon	1430	2000	Dushanbe	7J826 / 7J808	747SP
	Tue	1445	2100	Dushanbe	7J829 / 7J802	747SP
	Fri	1445	2100	Dushanbe	7J824 / 7J800	747SP
Dushanbe (DYU) - London (LHR)	Mon	1640	2000		7J808	747SP
	Tue	1740	2100		7J802	747SP
	Fri	1740	2100		7J800	747SP
	Sat	1740	2100		7J806	747SP
Karachi (KHI) - London (LHR)	Sat	1430	2100	Dushanbe	7J831 / 7J806	747SP
Yerevan (EVN) - London (LHR)	Sun	1730	2000	Dushanbe	7J810	747SP

* Following day

7

As outlined above, there were other details necessary for the operation. For the aircraft, copies of the In-Flight magazine and emergency information cards were printed and are illustrated below:

A WELCOME TO TAJIKISTAN
FROM THE PRIME MINISTER

It is with great pleasure and gratitude that I greet you in the first issue of the inflight magazine which will be distributed to passengers travelling to our country. Creation of the "air bridge" between Heathrow, London and Tajikistan is an event of huge importance for us. Regular international flights will be performed on this route by Tajik Air from now on. This shows the determination of our young, independent state to develop business links and cooperation on the international level, to maximise its economic, scientific and cultural potential, and to participate in the progress of mankind.

The people of our republic have undergone hard trials in the last two years. Civil war and natural disasters have caused unprecedented economic and moral damage. Today we are healing the wounds of the civil war and recovering the destroyed economy. Great amounts of money will be necessary to resurrect the country's economy. The legitimately elected government of the Republic, striving towards national unity, seeks to stabilise the situation within the Republic, to affirm the security of the state and safety of its citizens, and to reach mutual understanding with the neighbouring countries.

The present period is a difficult one. We have to overcome financial, economic and social crisis which require not only concentration of all inner forces but also the support of the world community.

Abdumalik Abdullajanov
Chairman of the
Council of Ministers of
Tajikistan.

Our future is clearly tied together with that of the Russian Federation, Uzbeckistan, Kazakhstan and other CIS countries.

The USA, Great Britain, Switzerland, Japan, India, Turkey, Pakistan, France and other countries have declared their readiness to provide financial assistance to us. We are involved in many foreign business ventures. Investors from Asia, the Near and Middle East, Europe and North American countries have expressed significant interest towards opportunities in Tajikistan. We not only ask for help but also offer to our partners mutually beneficial cooperation.

Our mountainous country with its high rivers and rich mineral deposits, in which there are more than 300 sunny days a year, has every thing to offer such opportunities.

I think that regular international flights will strengthen international business links.

Friends, you are welcome to our hospitable Tajik land.

A message from Michael Wynne-Parker
Honorary Consul for the Republic of Tajikistan
in the United Kingdom

The inauguration of scheduled Air Services between the United Kingdom and Tajikistan is historic and timely. Historic as the first ever Boeing 747 flies into Dushanbe! Timely as the services of Tajik Air provide the direct access to Tajikistan and Central Asia, both for the business man and the tourist - and both categories are growing in number daily.

Above all the beginning of this service symbolises that most important quality in todays troubled world - **FRIENDSHIP BETWEEN OUR NATIONS.**

Have a happy flight.

Inflight Entertainment

FEATURE FILM

ORLANDO

From: Jaguar Distribution (International)
Running Time: 93 minutes
Originally Rated: PG
Featuring: Tilda Swinton, Lothaire Bluteau, Billy Zane, Charlotte Valandrey, Heathcote Williams
Director: Sally Porter
Release Date: July 1993

An exciting and witty adaptation of Virginia Woolf's classic novel, ORLANDO.

Orlando is the story of a journey through time, of a man who lives four hundred years. As a young, wealthy nobleman, Orlando travels from the court of Queen Elizabeth I, across the frozen river Thames in 1610 to the deserts of central Asia. There in the midst of war, unwilling to kill or be killed, he is transformed into a woman. And so, Orlando returns to 18th century London where she faces a choice: marry or lose everything. In the Victoria age, a time of wildness and repression, she faces the loss of both love and inheritance.

Finally Orlando emerges into the present - a twentieth century of speed and noise ... as a person who, in losing everything, has gained her individuality.

FEATURE FILM

MARRIED TO IT

From: Orion Pictures
Running Time: 111 minutes
Originally Rated: R
Featuring: Beau Bridges, Stockard Channing, Robert Sean Leonard, Mary Stuart Masterson, Cybill Shepherd, Ron Silver
Director: Arthur Hiller
Release Date: March 1993

In "Married To It", the friendships - not to mention marriages - or three very different New York couples result in unexpected and often hilarious predicaments.

Leo Rothenberg and Claire Laurent (Ron Silver and Cybill Shepherd), John and Iris Morden (Beau Bridges and Stockard Channing), and Chuck and Nina Bishop (Robert Sean Leonard and Mary Stuart Masterson) are couples who meet while planning a pageant to be held at the private school attended by Leo's temperamental daughter, Lucy, and the Mordens' two teenaged sons. These diverse couples, each with their own problems and expectations, form a remarkable friendship as they begin to trust and believe in each other.

AUDIO PROGRAMME

Channel 2

Tajik Air F.M.
(Contemporary and classic rock)

Channel 3

Tajik Air "In Concert"
(Light/popular classics)

Channel 4

Favourites from Tajikistan
(A programme of popular music from our home)

Channel 5

Melodies from India
(A programme of favourites from India)

Channel 6/7

Easy listening
(music for relaxation)

All programmes 60 minutes in length. The Film Channel will be announced by the stewardess.

VIEWS OF TAJIKISTAN - THE LAND OF UNEXPLORED OPPORTUNITIES

Traditional Dancing

The Opera House

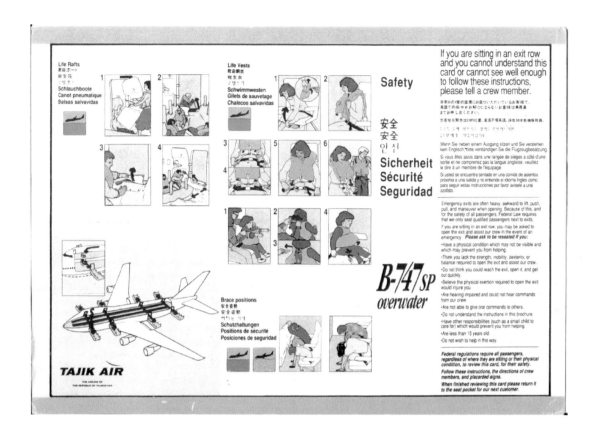

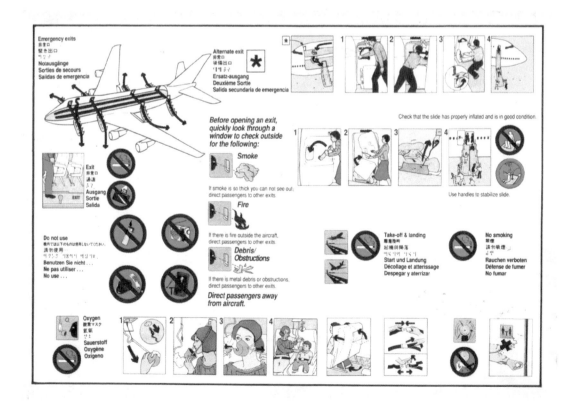

Additionally, as part of the pre-launch publicity, an article was put in a magazine for business travelers about the new service:

NEW SERVICE

ONE of the newest airlines offering services out of London's Heathrow Airport is Tajik Air, the airline of the Republic of Tajikistan, a Central Asian country north of Afghanistan and formerly part of the Soviet Union.

Tajik Air has been operating a B747SP out of Heathrow's Terminal 3 since the beginning of December 1993 with a three times weekly service to the Tajikistan capital, Dushanbe, with onward connections to Kojand also in Tajikistan – as well as to Karachi in Pakistan and Inida's capital, Delhi.

Flights depart from Heathrow each Thursday, Friday and Sunday at 22.15 returning from Dushanbe at 14.00 on Fridays, Saturdays and Mondays to reach Heathrow at 21.00 the same day. Flight timings are six hours eastbound and six hours 45 minutes westbound.

FOUR CLASSES

Tajik Air's B747SP carries 244 passengers in a four class configuration. Eighteen seats are available in First Class, 16 in Club Class, 18 in Economy de Luxe and 192 in Economy. Fares range from £870 for a return excursion (valid for up to three months) up to a First Class return fare of a little under £2,500.

ON-BOARD SERVICES

Tajik Air offers a full meal service on all its ex-London flights and also features 12 channels of audio as well as current films. Duty-free purchases are also available on board.

THE FUTURE

April 1994 sees the next phase of Tajik Air's route expansion when flights are introduced to Bangkok followed by Tokyo and Shanghai. Later in the year flights to the USA are expected to start commencing with Los Angeles. Tajikistan's 'most favoured nation' status is giving the national airline rights to fly to six destinations within the USA.

The airline was formed just two years ago with services to Karachi and Delhi and has enjoyed dramatic growth since then. High load factors have been achieved on ex-Heathrow services since day one with a substantial proportion of mainly business UK passengers.

For reservations or further information, please contact your GBTA agent or call Tajik Air on 071-937 7733.

For ticket sales, an office was set up in Kensington, London and a general sales agent was appointed in Karachi and Delhi. In addition, a large poster was printed for display at the ticketing offices with an image of Snow Leopard in the air:

The next steps in the launch of Tajik Air's new service to London involved recruiting and training flight crews and taking delivery of the aircraft.

Chapter II

Crew Training and Acceptance Flight

Crew Training

THE NEXT STEP IN GETTING *SNOW LEOPARD* into operation was getting a crew together to fly the Boeing 747SP. Because of the aircraft selection and their availability, it was decided to hire former pilots of Pan American World Airways. The decision was perfectly logical in that Pan Am pilots had many hours of experience in the 747SP – some had actually flown the aircraft when it was with Pan Am – had experience operating in the geographic area of the intended operation and had the savvy and know-how in dealing with unexpected circumstances or conditions that would be inherent in such an operation.

Captain Carr, a very experienced Pan Am pilot was one who received a call from a former colleague about an opportunity to be "an aviation pioneer again". According to Captain Carr, the offer was to operate a new 747 service for the former Soviet Socialist Republic of Tajikistan. He was told the route to be flown and that the pay would be minimal but with generous per diem and off-time. After some research he made his decision. He learned that Tajikistan

> ". . .is magnificently beautiful with a major fertile valley with a mild climate that grows cotton surrounded by majestic peaks rising 18 to 20 thousand feet and populated by their national symbol, the snow leopard. I also learned that (the capital) Dushanbe is on the old "Silk Road" route used by Marco Polo when he brought back to Italy, the secrets of making spaghetti from China. The neighboring cities of Tashkent and Samarkand conjured up images of wondrous bazaars and really old-world treasures of the Mongol Empire and kabobs made from Yak. I was hooked. Like the line from the Clint Eastwood movie: "do you feel lucky?" I did. I called back and signed up"

It was the same for all the pilots who received "the call". A chance to be an aviation pioneer was too great an opportunity to turn down.

Once the group was assembled, refresher training was arranged at the Pan Am International Flight Academy in Miami, Florida. The pilots were former Pan Amers and most were over 60 years of age. While that would present a problem in the United States, it did not for Tajikistan. And as is well known, pilots over the age of 60 have a near zero accident rate.

At the academy was a 747SP simulator and the pilots were put through a rigorous training program that brought them up to speed on changes to the aircraft, flight rules and fined-tuned their instrument piloting skills. At the same time, flight attendants from Tajik Air were undergoing training for the 747SP. These flight attendants were supposedly the "cream of the crop" from Tajik Air but with experience limited to smaller aircraft such as the TU-154 (an old 3-engine aircraft that looked remarkably like at Boeing 727).

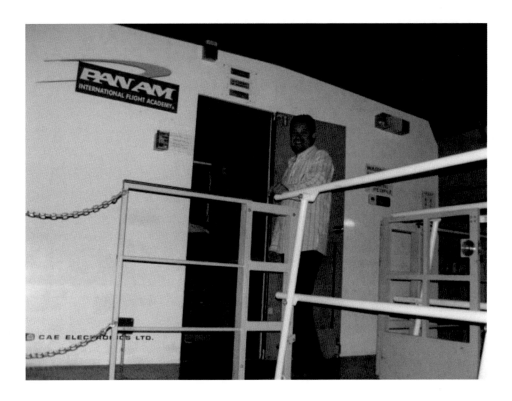

While the pilots were progressing well in the refresher training, it was not the case for the flight attendants.

A former Pan Am purser, Gunilla Crawford, was working in contracts at the Pan Am Flight Academy when she received word that the Tajik Air flight attendants were to receive training on the 747SP. Upon their arrival, she immediately discovered a serious problem: their English-speaking ability was extremely limited! According to Purser Crawford:

"I had created a training program for the Tajik flight attendants, and we started with the 747SP aircraft: the doors, how to arm, disarm, open and close in normal and emergency mode. The first day was spent studying the manual; the second day in the mock- up; the third day back in the classroom. But I soon realized it would take five days to learn the doors and it would take months to teach procedures.

"Nothing I tried worked with the students, mainly because of the language barrier, and partly because of the size of the aircraft. The 747SP had two aisles vs. the TU-154 single aisle; oxygen masks in the overhead on the747SP vs. two 5" tall oxygen tanks in the aft of the TU-154 cabin, held in place on the floor, standing up! (When we had a delay in Dushanbe, I went onboard and saw the difference.)"

A flight academy employee who spoke Russian eventually acted as an interpreter, but it became painfully clear that this group would not be able to staff a 747SP. Although kind, interested and friendly, they were overwhelmed by the size of the 747SP.

This problem was not only a concern to Purser Crawford, but also to the pilots who were undergoing refresher training at the same time and who had observed the Tajik flight attendants firsthand. A solution to the problem was needed, and according to Captain Carr, after meeting with aviation officials from Tajikistan who were present, it was decided to hire some "real" flight attendants from the former Pan Am. Purser Crawford was in contact with a group of "experienced and adventurous" former cabin crew colleagues, and very soon thereafter, a lot of familiar faces began appearing at the Pan Am Flight Academy.

Training went into full swing for all concerned and soon it was finished. For the cabin crew, it was decided that two or three experienced Pan Am flight attendants would be assigned to each flight. The remaining cabin crew positions would be filled by the Tajik Air flight attendants as "trainees". The goal, under the supervision and direction of the Pan Am crew, was the Tajik crew to become qualified to "staff and run" a 747SP flight.

However, there was one more thing: Teamwork.

Captain Carr:

> *"Being on a flight crew is a wonderful thing. It is a team effort. Pan Am had always encouraged working as a team. That teamwork was designed to save lives. Although the duties of the cabin staff are the care and feeding of passengers, their real job is to save lives in an emergency. They operate the emergency equipment and are trained to get people out of the aircraft as quickly as possible. Good communication is essential. As a pilot, I have always appreciated and respected the job the flight attendants do and made sure they knew it".*

In observing the training of the Tajik flight attendants, good communication was non-existent. To alleviate this problem, Captain Carr suggested the Tajiks should see more of America other than their hotel and the flight academy and invited them and his fellow pilots to a luncheon at his home. During the luncheon he made a very important observation:

> *"[At] almost any cookout in America, guests would pitch in to help with the food and drinks and have a party. Not so with the Tajiks. It became apparent that the concept of initiative did not exist in their culture. They would smile and do anything we asked of them but took no initiative. In an airplane emergency, this can be deadly so we proceeded to see what we could do about it. This was the first chance the pilots and cabin staff had the opportunity to talk in an informal setting. We encouraged them to help themselves and to pass things along to their fellow crewmembers.*

> *"We also started to find out why they didn't talk to each other. They were all from Tajikistan, but some were from various mountain tribes that were at odds with each other. Others were Russian, or Iranian or Tajik valley people. Apparently, they had been chosen not because of their good English or flying experience but because they were related to government officials. This was also meant to be a representative group of the Tajik population. While I thought this was a very democratic move, I later learned this diversity was meant to make it less likely that a jealous faction would [cause problems with the operation].*

> *"The lunch went very well and the English phrases, "more beer", "more vodka" were pronounced much better. I also made arrangements to charter*

a water taxi for a cruise to see the Bahia Mar Yachting Center and also homes along the waterway. [At the end of the tour] and before returning to Miami, the Tajiks stopped by our home to thank us. Much to my relief they were now all smiling and talking to each other and acting like a flight crew. That lunch was one of the best investments I ever made."

With the training finished and the Tajiks fresh from their team-building experience, everyone began leaving Miami for London to start the operation. Captain Carr was asked to make the "acceptance flight" of *Snow Leopard*. He accepted.

Acceptance Flight

The acceptance flight is a critical part of the delivery process of an aircraft to an airline. Once the aircraft is accepted and delivered, anything that is discovered wrong with the aircraft becomes the responsibility of the airline. Inspections and the acceptance flight should ensure that this does not happen. *Snow Leopard* was flown to London by a United Airlines supervisory pilot and crew. Upon arrival, Captain Carr and his crew met the aircraft and began the task of inspecting the aircraft, its logs and maintenance records and carrying out the acceptance flight. The aircraft looked great with a fresh paint job with Tajik Air livery. Once everything was signed off, and the walk-around inspection complete, the aircraft was pronounced airworthy, and Captain Carr and his crew boarded the aircraft to begin the flight.

However, once on board, there was a surprise awaiting them: The aircraft was full of people! Normally such a flight involves the necessary minimum crew members. Not this one. The press was on board, as were Tajik Air officials, the Minister of Aviation of Tajikistan and management staff. In fact, station personnel and baggage handlers were also on board!

Captain Carr:

"[I had] a quiet conversation with the [Minister of Aviation] to make sure that carrying all these people on a test flight was okay. I learned that wonderful Russian phrase: 'kharasho' ('no problem'). Since he was the law for our Tajikistan operating certificate, it was like getting the word directly from God.

"I climbed into my seat in the cockpit. The United pilot looked really nervous and seemed a few shades deeper red than normal. He indicated his concern

about all these people on board, and I said 'kharasho', took the clip board from him and signed as Pilot in Command. He looked relieved. I reminded him that United was still responsible for any maintenance items until I signed the aircraft acceptance form. The flight went smoothly, the aircraft was perfect, and everyone enjoyed the tour of the English countryside as we put the airplane through its paces. We returned to Heathrow and I made my first landing in a real 747 in about a year and a half. As we came in on final approach, I realized that we had almost all the top brass aboard, the new crewmembers and a whole planeload of people who had never been on a 747 before.

"If you're flying a 747 correctly, on speed and according to 'the book', it normally makes a very nice landing. Once in a while, when conditions are just right and you are very lucky, the touch down is so smooth that you don't realize you are on the ground until the speedbrake handle comes up as it automatically reacts to a microswitch on the landing gear as the wheels touch ground. This was one of those landings.

"It is a Russian custom to applaud after a landing. But I did not think this applause was for landing, rather giving thanks to be alive. However, during the flight we kept the door open for the bigwigs to view the cockpit and after landing I heard the cheers and applause from behind. Winning an Oscar for an actor couldn't feel any better than how that landing and applause felt to me. As we all left the aircraft my new bosses kept congratulating me as though I was the greatest pilot in the world. What could I say? I just smiled and secretly thanked Boeing."

Gunilla Crawford, having arrived in London to handle flight service, also had a look at *Snow Leopard* prior to delivery:

"The day came when we were to see the plane for the first time. It was a rainy overcast day, but there she was as beautiful as ever, sitting on the wet tarmac. We inspected the galleys, the equipment and planned the last details, now that a few months of training and planning had come together, and the real adventure was to begin. 'Starving' for flying since the demise of Pan Am . . .we were all raring to go, as this would be the 'real' thing......or so we thought."

It was now time to get ready for operations. Ticket sales and crew scheduling were at the top of the agenda.

Chapter III

The Inaugural Flight

Selling Tickets

WITH THE ACCEPTANCE FLIGHT COMPLETED and the aircraft ready to start operations, management and staff got into full gear. Tickets were sold, crews scheduled, and plans were made for launch activities. At the London Headquarters on Kensington High Street, tickets sales in both the Delhi, India and Karachi, Pakistan markets was brisk, and flights sold out very quickly. However, ticket sales in the Dushanbe market were slow due to very little western business activity in the country, and what little passenger traffic there was, was largely government in nature. Thus, selling seats in the beyond markets was necessary. As described in Part One, this "Sixth Freedom" operation enabled a profit on what would have been money losing flights. In fact, over 90-95% of the booked passengers were booked on flights to Delhi or Karachi. Deeply discounted advance purchase excursion tickets offered through local travel agents in the ethnic neighborhoods of London resulted in a huge response.

The Kensington High Street Headquarters served as both a ticket office and operations base with constant activity, day and night. This was punctuated with welcome and frequent visits by the Pan Am and Tajik flight crews.

Ticket Sales at Kensington High Street Office

Tajik Staff

Pan Am Flight Crews visiting Kensington High Street Headquarters

Cabin Crew Scheduling

While ticket sales and preparations for the inaugural flight were progressing, Gunilla Crawford and her team of flight attendants set about to organize crew scheduling and rotations. This was no easy task!

Cabin crew scheduling was a challenge for Gunilla. With no computers available, some creativity was required:

Gunilla Crawford:

"We went across the street from the hotel to a gas station and bought four dinosaur-shaped erasers in four different colors. Each dinosaur represented a crew. And each crew consisted of two ex-Pan Am flight attendants and the rest Tajik. On a large poster board, we plotted the four destinations, London, Dushanbe, Karachi, and New Delhi. By moving the dinosaurs between the destinations, we made sure nobody was scheduled from London, when in fact the crew member was in New Delhi!"

24

(left to right) Gunilla Crawford, Vince Rossi and Debbie Thornburg

(left to right) Gunilla Crawford, Linda Morehouse and Vince Rossi - note the colored dinosaurs!

and . . . Catering

When Gunilla arrived in London, she was in for a surprise. In addition to heading up the cabin crew, there was another responsibility as well: Catering. She handled that in pure Pan Am fashion.

"We made appointments with Catering at Heathrow airport, we picked china for the First Class Service, silverware, serving dishes, baskets and linens. The "old" Pan Am training came back in force and we would do the service in the name of that classic carrier."

The food service to be offered was superb.

In First Class departing London, "Royal Doulton Service" included during the drinks service a choice of Hot Canapes including Chicken Kebab, Mushroom Cream Vol-au-Vent, Spring Roll, Basil Cashew Parmesan Tartlets and Asian Canapes of mixed pakoras and samosas. The Hors d'oeuvres offered a choice of Poached Salmon Medallion on Oakleaf lettuce with Diced Pepper and Cucumber Salad, or a Tomato Cup filled with Mayonnaise Lemon garnish or a Smoked Chicken Breast on Radicchio with Mandarin Orange and Cucumber or a Radish and Mixed Peppers Julienne, all with a Mixed Leaf Salad with Vinaigrette. For the entree, the choices were Curry Prawn Jalfrezi with fresh chopped Coriander, Rack of Lamb with Herbs and Fresh Rosemary Sprigs or Chicken Shirin Polo accompanied by Basmati Rice with Zereshk or Potato Sesame Croquettes and a choice of vegetables including Broccoli au Gratin Mornay or Steamed Mixed Vegetables with Baby Sweetcorn, Turned Carrots and Mange Tout.

For desert Gateau Chocolate Roulade with Orange Zest was followed by a cheese plate that included Camembert, Port Salut, Feta, Stilton, Brie with black grapes, black and green olives and celery batons. Ending the meal was a fresh fruit basket.

Prior to landing in Dushanbe, the pre-arrival "hot breakfast was just as posh...It was like working the Pan Am *Clippers* again", according to Vince Rossi one of the ex-Pan Am flight attendants.

The Inaugural Flight

As the day approached for *Snow Leopard's* first revenue flight from London to Dushanbe and onwards to Karachi, the crews began assembling in London to prepare. For Gunilla, it was a happy reunion with the Tajik flight attendants who greeted their ex-Pan Am counterparts with "squeals and shouts of joy". For the inaugural flight four ex-Pan Am were to work the flight, Robert Stewart, Tania Anderson, Linda Morehouse and Linda Oja. On the flight deck were Captain Ed Olasz, First Officer Jim Donahue and Flight Engineer Carl Meixal. In addition, two qualified captains were assigned to the flight.

Preparations for departure went into high gear. Nothing was overlooked. Everything was covered, from the accuracy of the manuals to training to CRM (crew resources management) with the Tajik flight attendants. Anything that could possibly happen, even the unpredictable, was discussed and thoroughly prepared for.

The excitement of flying again did not escape the ex-Pan Amers who were taking part in the operation. *Snow Leopard's* first flight coincided almost to the date of the demise of their beloved Pan Am, some two years prior.

Tania Anderson:

> "I happily scribbled away in my diary, gushing about the thrill of flying with my cosmopolitan colleagues again. A few fondly remembered having flown with this particular 747SP before. Some of my co-workers had not flown since Pan Am's demise. It had been nearly two years to the day that I had been on my last flight, a White House Press Charter, when we learned that we were bankrupt for good. Now as we gathered in the lobby of our London hotel for the first flight to Dushanbe, we all noted the sad anniversary coupled with the excitement of exploring a new airline together."

At 2215 hrs. on the date of the inaugural flight, *Snow Leopard*, designated 7J801, departed London Heathrow for Dushanbe. The spirit on board was one of joy and happiness.

Tania Anderson:

> "During the flight, I quickly noted that many of the passengers, who were going onto Karachi, were much less frenetic than the ones we used to fly on Pan Am. They were elated to be going home, either for a visit or permanently, for a reasonably priced airline ticket. One passenger asked if he could kiss me, and I reluctantly replied, 'Well, Ok, but on my cheek!' I also noted in my diary that we were flying across Russian airspace which may not sound

like a big deal but to someone who grew up during the Cold War when the former USSR was our mortal enemy, it was intriguing to me.

"The multi-national crew also bonded quickly. The Tajik flight attendants loved the fact that my name was Tania. Naturally assuming that I was Russian with a name like Tania, one actually commented that I spoke good fluent English for a Russian. Some of the Tajiks were dark with olive skin and Middle Eastern looks. Most were Muslim. Others were the opposite end of the spectrum with white skin and light eyes. They were usually Russian Orthodox.

"Among the Tajik flight attendants, there were three Irenas on the flight. Any time I said 'Irena', all three would whirl around simultaneously to see what I wanted. The Tajik flight attendants were absolutely delightful and so easy to get along with. They were also thrilled to have secured a job such as this with the opportunity to explore a bit of the world, especially London. Many of them had no transportation from their homes, so they simply walked miles to the airport to work these extraordinarily long flights. They went out of their way to tell us how their country was still in a lot of upheaval economically. In addition, Afghani insurgents were coming over the border to make trouble, and they wanted none of it. 'Tania, we just all want peace and to be able to live our lives', one told me."

The Pan Am and Tajik Flight Crews

After a long flight into the night, *Snow Leopard* landed in Dushanbe.

Tania Anderson:

> *"It was a cold, wintry, snowy day when we landed in Dushanbe to a zealous reception on the tarmac. After all, we were the first western aircraft to ever land in somewhat remote Tajikistan. I distinctly remember applause in the cabin upon our touchdown, but the local hoopla outside just about had me abandoning my jump-seat.*
>
> *"With a dramatic back drop of steep snow-encrusted mountains, dozens of well-wishers had gathered on the tarmac in their traditional brightly-colored clothes. There was a band playing Russian instruments complete with long-nosed horns and big drums. Tajik national TV was there with their ancient equipment to record every single minute of the ceremonies and our arrival."*

The Reception at Dushanbe Airport

Tania Anderson:

"Once on the blocks, the ground people enthusiastically boarded the plane, not only to welcome us, but to ask for a quick tour of the 747SP. Descending the spiral staircase, our pilots were given handsome home-made colorful robes to wear over their uniforms. Now that the door was open, I could observe the entire scene. Our pilots were quickly ushered down the stairs and off to the terminal for a reception including some local culinary treats whose identity was left to the imagination. Later one of them told me that the Tajiks had insisted that they shoot some vodka—maybe local moonshine—to celebrate the day. A bit horrified, our pilots made certain that the officials knew we still had another leg to fly to Karachi, but the general response was like, 'So what?'

"Linda Oja and I stayed on the plane watching everything from L-1. Then something happened I shall never forget. As Linda squealed, 'Oh, No!' I saw some Tajiks dragging a sheep across the tarmac towards the Snow Leopard. It struggled the entire way, right up to the staircase, just as if it knew something lousy was about to occur. As they do in many countries, they sacrificed the sheep at the bottom of our stairs, directing the blood from his neck into a bowl. In the west we christen ships and airplanes with

champagne, but now we were halfway around the world in a land with customs very different than our own.

"Not long afterwards, the entire crew along with the ground people gathered in front of the aircraft for a memorable photo. Each of us was festooned with garlands of deep, red-colored roses. They were velvet to the touch and their fragrance was heavenly, even against the cold blast of mid-winter."

Tania Anderson:

"Standing there on that frosty winter day, I felt a true sense of pride about our latest 'operation'. In true Pan Am fashion, we had pulled ourselves up after the bankruptcy and were on the other side of the planet helping the struggling Tajiks with their burgeoning airline, begun with one beautiful 747SP.

"Flying on the Snow Leopard *was another wonderful Pan Amigo adventure to add to my memoirs."*

When Snow Leopard arrived at Dushanbe that wintery morning, Tajikistan was amid an economic crisis along with a civil war. Bread was being rationed but at the same time the country was trying to turn the page into a new chapter of their existence, emerging from the era of Soviet rule to an independent and free nation. The arrival of this beautiful 747SP representing their national airline stoked both great pride and happiness among its citizens.

Chapter IV

What Could Have Been

THE STORY OF *SNOW LEOPARD* from the beginning was the story of a revolutionary idea that should have been hugely successful. Unfortunately the fates would not allow that and countless hours of devotion to a noble project went to waste. If there is blame, it is not worth dwelling on. Everyone wanted the right outcome. Unfortunately, it was not to be.

Nevertheless, the London staff, pilots and cabin crew worked their mightiest to make this project work, using initiative and self-sacrifice to get over what eventually became an insurmountable problem.

Once the regular schedule was established and operating, the flights still presented a challenge to everyone involved and it goes without saying they were up to it. The Pan Am culture in which the pilots and flight attendants grew up lent itself to innovation and decisiveness in dealing with the everyday issues they confronted while operating *Snow Leopard*. A case in point are the experiences of Captain Carr, who encountered his share of challenges during his first trip as Pilot-in-Command on *Snow Leopard*.

Flying Snow Leopard to Delhi and Back

Captain Carr, who flew the acceptance flight, arrived in London for his first revenue trip and met with the rest of the flight crews at his hotel who briefed him on the operation. He also learned that the flights for the next two months were full, "which was a relief to me as I was anxious for my new employers to succeed". That evening, he reported with his crew to London's Heathrow Airport for his trip to Delhi with a short stop in Dushanbe. While completing pre-flight, which included verifying the flight plan, the weather, the fuel load, the passenger load, weight and balance and reviewing the current Notice to Airmen, he learned that the flight was being handled by United Airlines Dispatch in Chicago.

Captain Carr:

"I reported to the aircraft with my crew and was greeted warmly by the Tajik Air Station Manager and his wife. I briefed the flight service team about our flight time (6 1/2 hours to Dushanbe; 2 1/2 hours to Delhi) and conducted a review of emergency procedures. I checked with catering and baggage handling to ensure things were progressing for an on-time departure. All was well. So far.

"The cockpit of a 747 is on the top deck making it difficult to observe the loading progress. So, one relies on clues such as all doors closing but one, or the tug getting ready for push-back. As our departure time neared, these things weren't happening. I could see through the window into the boarding area and saw a huddle of ground personnel talking on cell phones. I contacted flight-ops by radio and found that the United Airlines Dispatch Center had not sent the final weight and balance figures. I said: 'So what. We have the figures here; we can finish it.' 'That's not the way we do it', said the United London ops man. We waited at the gate 45 minutes until someone in Chicago sent us our final weight and balance based on the numbers we sent them. I said 'hmmnnn' and made a couple of notes."

The flight was finally cleared and took off for Dushanbe. For Captain Carr, it was "great to be flying again". The route took *Snow Leopard* over Belgium, Germany, and Czechoslovakia, and across the former Soviet Union. In the flight deck, the pilots were busy with position reports, weather updates and programming the waypoints on the route into the Inertial Navigation System (INS) on the aircraft. This system directs the flight as it moves along its route. Connected to autopilot, it makes piloting the flight effortless. Except in the former Soviet Union.

Captain Carr:

"The airways in the USSR were established when airplanes flew about 100 mph with reporting points very close together and in zig zag courses that were established by radio beacons installed along winding roads or rivers that were only accessible by mule or boat. The result was that we found ourselves barely able to stay ahead of the aircraft progress while loading the many way points. We asked the Russian ground controllers if we could fly a straighter route and report every hundred miles or so but this was 1993 and they were still very strict about enforcing their old ways."

The flight, however, made good progress and was on its way for an on-time arrival. Then there was a problem: Fluid loss in one of the hydraulic systems that required an alternative procedure to lower the landing gear and made the nose wheel steering inoperative. This was "no big whoop" to Captain Carr. These were things pilots were trained to deal with. The landing in Dushanbe was routine and Captain Carr requested a tug to tow the aircraft to the gate.

Captain Carr:

"'What tug?' the tower responded. It turns out there was no tug at Dushanbe capable of moving a 747. The book says you can't taxi a 747 without the # 1 hydraulic system which is the one we lost, but, as an old Navy Pilot used to a carrier aircraft that didn't have nose wheel steering anyway, we just went back to basics. Using differential brakes and forward thrust on one side and idle reverse on the other we swung right around and taxied up to the terminal. 'Kharasho' ('no problem'). The Dushanbe passengers deplaned, and we asked everyone else to stay on board while we examined the situation."

After examining the landing gear, the source of the leak was identified and capped. Repairs would be done in Delhi. The crew determined that the aircraft could continue to Delhi with the landing gear locked down adding about 45 minutes to the flight plan, arriving in Delhi a little late. Communications in Dushanbe, however, was quite primitive, and after several unsuccessful attempts by the operations office to contact London and Chicago, Captain Carr finally reached Chicago by HF frequency from the aircraft. He explained the situation and got his first taste of United Corporate Culture.

Captain Carr:

"'You can't do that,' said the United dispatcher in Chicago. 'We don't have any such procedure for gear down flights with passengers.' I explained we had such procedures and that our operating certificate was based on using Pan Am manuals, flight procedures and techniques and the manuals permitted safe operation with the gear down. We had been doing it since the introduction of the first 747. I asked him: 'Don't you realize that every flight operates with the gear down at the beginning and end? We were just going to have it down longer.' He said he didn't care, he had checked with his bosses and if we attempted to fly with the gear down, they would repossess

the aircraft. I had to give the bad news to the local Tajik Air people and two managers from London who were with us. We had to come up with plan B".

The next problem for Captain Carr was dealing with the passengers still on board going to Delhi. There were no hotels available to put them up overnight. Also, the aircraft heating and electricity was being powered by an on-board auxiliary power unit (APU) that used up fuel and there was no fuel available in Dushanbe. If the APU was kept running, there would not be enough fuel for the flight to Delhi. In addition, the airport was closing, and airport personnel were going home.

Captain Carr:

"The local Tajik Air managers came up with the idea of using one of their Tupolev 154s, which could carry our passengers but not their luggage. The Tupolev crew was called to the airport, their airplane readied, and I was told all we had to do was transfer our passengers to the other aircraft. I learned that wasn't going to be so easy.

"In London, the BBC had been reporting on the theft of airline baggage. Most of the passengers were Indian Nationals, many of whom carrying as many VCRs, portable TVs and other small appliances as their luggage would bear. When I told them that they would be continuing to Delhi on the Tupolev, but could not take their luggage, there was a near riot. A few began wagging their fingers in my face. I asked the Hindi speaking members of our crew to translate for me so there would be no misunderstanding. I explained there were no hotel rooms, that we had to shut down our aircraft and if they tried to stay, they would freeze to death. I told them we had made arrangements to get them to their destination and their luggage would be arriving the next morning. Their response was underwhelming. To emphasize our security arrangements, I had our guards come aboard the airplane and hold their Kalashnikov machine guns over their heads to show our passengers that their luggage would be well protected. These were not ordinary airport security guards but members of the élite Russian Spetsnaz. I was very glad to see them providing security. And having them behind me to back up my promise to protect the passengers' luggage worked very well. Also, no one else wagged a finger in my face.

"The Tupolev was brought along side and the passengers began filing from one aircraft to the other in the dark. Once the transfer was complete, I went

to the Tupolev to meet the cockpit crew and wish our passengers a bon voyage. I introduced myself to the captain and his crew. We chatted a bit and their Captain smiled and said: 'Don't worry Captain, we'll take good care of your passengers and crew.' I was grateful for his recognizing my concern and addressing it. I was very impressed. I thanked him and went through the cabin thanking all the passengers for their cooperation. I also thanked all our flight service team for all their hard work during a difficult time. They were terrific."

After spending the night at a hotel in Dushanbe, Captain Carr and his crew returned to Dushanbe Airport to find a "pile of papers that truly impressed me" and that "United in Chicago. . .had come to the conclusion" that he was right and released the aircraft for a ferry flight to Delhi with gear down.

Captain Carr:

"We boarded the airplane and took off. It was a beautiful day and even with the gear down the SP climbed easily to cross the Hindu Kush and surrounding peaks that rose to about 24,000 feet. We were enjoying the scenery as we cruised at 29,000 feet entering Pakistan. We made our position report to the Pakistan air controller who asked us to confirm our country of registration. No one could believe that Tajikistan had a 747. He asked us for our overflight permit number. Before take-off we had received our en-route clearance, but no one had said anything about an overflight permit number. I hadn't heard of this before and in my years of flying with Pan Am, had never been asked for one. The three of us in the cockpit began searching through the paperwork. I began reading the controller numbers we found but they were not the number he wanted. He sounded very unhappy and eventually his supervisor radioed: 'Tajik Air 801, you have entered Pakistani airspace illegally and are directed to land at Lahore Airport immediately.' I explained that we were a ferry flight because of a mechanical difficulty and that it would be dangerous to divert and could not comply. He said: 'You must land immediately.' I again explained that I am using my authority as Captain for the safety of my aircraft and crew to proceed. We only had about 5 more minutes until we were out of Pakistan Airspace. I pushed the throttles up as much as I dared and we kept looking out both sides and hoped that if they scrambled fighters, that they would at least do one fly-by before shooting at us. We reached the Indian/Pakistan border, and I thanked the Pakistan air controller for his 'cooperation'.

"We landed at Delhi and taxied to the gate where I could see the smiling passengers looking out the big windows as they waited to get their luggage. Entering the terminal, I spoke with our Senior Purser and mentioned again how glad I was to have thought of the idea of having the Spetsnaz show off their weapons to assure the passengers that their belongings would be well protected. She said: 'Oh no Captain. They didn't get off the plane because they thought you were protecting their luggage. They got off because they thought you were going to shoot them.' I had wondered why the passengers moved so quickly out of my way as I walked down the ramp."

Pamir Mountains as seen from *Snow Leopard*

Captain Carr and his crew stayed in Delhi for a three-day layover, during which *Snow Leopard* made a London-Karachi rotation through Dushanbe. When *Snow Leopard* returned to Delhi, he and his crew would take it back to London. At Delhi Airport, he learned that the weather in Dushanbe was "iffy", adding the requirement of planning a fuel load so that they would be light enough to land in Dushanbe yet have enough to make it to London if they had to bypass Tajikistan. This was resolved by using a "re-dispatch" flight plan that provided for a fuel stop at an alternative airport if necessary.

Captain Carr:

"We took off on schedule with a full load of passengers, fortunately none bound for Tajikistan, because as we approached Dushanbe, we learned that it was snowing heavily, and the runway could not be cleared. We were then informed that we had to deviate north of Azerbaijan due to 'military activities'. All I could think of was, 'uh-oh, there goes our fuel and our on-time arrival in London'. The distance from Delhi to London is normally not a problem for a 747SP, but, because we had to limit the amount of fuel we could carry, we had the minimum amount to make it to London and now had to worry about using up our reserves. However, our calculations indicated that we would still have the proper amount of reserve fuel.

"As we progressed west, the weather reports for London kept getting worse. We were advised by Maastricht Control, (Netherlands), that there were delays for aircraft inbound to Heathrow. We had now been airborne for almost nine hours and were getting close to the minimum fuel that would let us safely proceed to our alternate airport. We were told to enter the holding pattern at Lamborne, less than 20 miles from London's Heathrow Airport. I knew it could take up to an hour or more to cover those last 20 miles. We were flying in ovals on a specific flight path at a specific altitude separated by 1000 feet from the aircraft above and below. We were still at 16,000 feet and since the approach normally is not begun until we have worked our way down through the 'stack' to 8,000 feet I knew we were going to be doing this for a while and it was quite possible that we would reach our 'bingo' fuel, the minimum amount left for us to proceed to our alternate airport. I excused myself and went aft for a stretch and briefed the senior purser that we might have to divert to Stansted Airport.

"When I returned to the cockpit, I was glad to see we had worked our way down to 12,000 feet. We had also been in continuous contact with our Flight Ops to check on Stansted weather. It was okay and the winds were favorable to get there. Nevertheless, I had to tell London Control that we could only make two more turns in the pattern and would then have to divert. At the very last moment, we had worked our way down and were cleared for an approach. The weather had gotten worse, and we were faced with zero ceiling and zero visibility, called a 'zero-zero landing'.

"A 747 can make zero-zero landing if the aircraft and airport are properly equipped, which they were. We committed to making a zero-zero landing, requiring an instrument approach. The aircraft flies where you want it to go with just a caress of the controls. For this landing I decided to make a 'coupled approach', on the auto pilot. Even though the autopilot is flying the airplane, the pilot still must follow all the instruments as though flying manually and keep hands on the controls to override just in case. I let the autopilot make the actual touch down and apply the brakes.

"One strange thing about a zero-zero landing is that after you land is when it gets dicey. The trick is to slow the aircraft and keep it on the runway that still can't be seen. Fortunately, on the runway are 'center line lights' embedded in the concrete. But though they are very bright, in low visibility, one can only see a couple at a time and the trick is to run over them with the nose wheel. Otherwise, if one loses sight of the lights, there is no way to tell if the aircraft is to the right or left, other than instinct, until it runs off the runway.

"Once the aircraft was slow enough, we used the 'lead-in lights' to our gate. Following the green lights embedded in the taxi ways and stopping when they turn red is all there is to it. Just before the last red stop light, we saw the bricks of the terminal. We had arrived."

Dushanbe Airport

The flight attendants also had interesting experiences. Vince Rossi recalls making "care" packages from the inbound catering overages for the pilots laying over in Dushanbe. The flight attendants would also set up a buffet for the ground staff and soldiers there. It was a big event whenever *Snow Leopard* arrived at Dushanbe. According to Rossi, "in spite of the bitter winter cold, there were often people watching from the terminal and nearby the airport".

There were other interesting aspects of operating through Dushanbe Airport. Capitalism flourished! At the time of the *Snow Leopard* operation, ground handling was handled by individual "small businesses", each performing a single function. Thus, the baggage handling was a "small business" and the worker was paid directly for his services. This was also the case for the passenger stairs, blocking, fueling, cleaning the aircraft, and other air-side activities. One interesting observation was the snow removal operation as described by former Pan Am Purser Gunilla Crawford:

> *"It was becoming cold and one of our concerns was the lack of de-icing equipment. We were the biggest plane they had ever seen in Dushanbe, and all they had was a three rung ladder and a mop!!!! We questioned the contents of the bucket, and decided it was probably Vodka. The wings they could reach from the left and right '3' doors inside the plane, but the tail was another issue. It was just way too high."*

Soon, a cherry-picker appeared to take care of the tail, and it, too, was a small business that was paid directly for its services.

Snowbound Dushanbe Airport

Layovers in Exotic Places

One of the attractions of working for an international airline is the opportunity to visit countries all over the world and explore them during layovers. Layovers are necessary to ensure flight crew members are not "timed out" and are well rested for their next segment.

In the case of Tajik Air, most layovers were in Delhi, where the hotels were plentiful and there were places to visit. Except, of course, when there is a major holiday, and the hotels are fully booked. This happened to Gunilla Crawford and her crew:

"We got to Delhi and decided to go to a hotel in the airport area, but every hotel was full. We agreed that we had indeed a hotel at the airport ourselves, our plane. 9 bathrooms, 3 galleys and plenty of seats, [and] in First Class the seats reclined pretty flat. For three days we stayed, parked in this cargo area, ordered food, walked on the tarmac for exercise and read books. "

Dushanbe was not considered a layover city, but there were times that a layover was necessary due to operational circumstances. For the most part, due to the political situation in Tajikistan, the flight attendants kindly declined the opportunity to sample Dushanbe. The pilots, however, did. Captain Carr's first layover was the overnighter, caused by the landing gear problem. This was his first experience in a former Soviet Republic.

Captain Carr:

"We watched the Tupolev taxi out and take off, secured our plane, set our departure for about 10 a.m. the next morning, waved goodbye to the guards and got on our bus to the hotel. As tired as I was, I was now looking forward to actually being in Dushanbe. Some of the Spetsnaz came with us on the bus and explained that we would be traveling after curfew and the roads were not necessarily free of problems. Problems? I didn't ask what problems. I was cool. Speaking of cool, the bus was very similar to an American school bus circa 1950 and if it was plus-10 F outside the bus, it was minus-10 inside. We finally made it to the hotel, and I was greatly relieved to see that it looked very nice. This was my first USSR hotel. We were greeted by a giant fellow in a caftan of sorts wearing a beautifully decorated hat that was a cross between a fez and a skull-cap. I didn't know whether to bow to him or shake his hand but he resolved this by taking our luggage. He was the combination bellman, guard and lobby bouncer. We were told the hotel was full but they would make some rooms available for us. I have never liked giving up my passport at a hotel desk but even though we were crew-members and accompanied by the Tajik Air Dushanbe Station Manager, we were told: 'no passport, no room.' I gave up my passport. I asked if we could get something to eat. 'Breakfast' was the

answer. 'Now?' I asked, 'Morning. No food now.' We received keys to our rooms and proceeded up in an elevator to our floor. I mentioned that the hotel looked nice from the outside. My first impression was that it may have also looked nice on the inside, but I wasn't absolutely sure because it was so dark."

The next time Captain Carr visited Dushanbe he had a chance to have a better view of the city. This was a city that was affected by the then ongoing civil war and things were quite unstable. The country was struggling, and its economy was to say the least, precarious.

Captain Carr:

"My next layover in Dushanbe gave me another jolt of realism. We made arrangements with the Station Manager to take a tour of the Dushanbe area. He was able to provide the same bus that took us to and from the hotel. We drove through some areas with some very grand government buildings with surprisingly attractive architecture. We stopped at a beautiful park with some magnificent statuary. It didn't take us too long to realize though that something was wrong. No people on the streets. No cars on the roads. The only other humans we saw on our drive were local policemen who stopped our bus, asked for our identification, and extracted a small 'toll' for passing through their section of road. I don't believe they received much else in the way of pay. We headed back to the area of our hotel and stopped at a 'super market.' It was quite a large store, larger than most in the U.S. but dramatically different. The shelves were all bare except for one corner of the store where a man dispensed potatoes into burlap bags with a shovel. This was the government store. We did finally find a 'people's market' with fresh vegetables and other marketable foods and goods. We were able to buy some tasty snacks and food to carry us through the evening curfew. I also made my one big purchase of a local item that is my one souvenir of my Tajikistan experience."

"On flights, we were all wearing our old Pan Am uniforms without the Pan Am insignia or hats. I thought it would be nice to have a hat with an emblem indicative of Tajikistan. I found the perfect thing on a peddler's cart. It was a pin-on gold medallion of a beautifully crafted snow leopard. I happily purchased it, stuck it on my beret, and it was my contribution to uniform design and a personal trademark thereafter. I took a little kidding at first but then all the other crewmembers wanted one as well.

"The next day, the Engineer, First Officer and I decided to walk over to explore another hotel that we had noticed not too far away. The hotel seemed very attractive from the outside. The lobby was very dark and deserted but after we rang a little bell on the main desk, a clerk eventually appeared. I asked if we could look around and see their rooms. 'Da'. He pointed to a doorway with a flight of stairs. We went up and came to what appeared to be an airport style security check point with a walk-through metal detector and guards with Kalashnikov machine guns. After we got through, we ran into a fellow on the upper landing that seemed to be an American. He asked if he could help us, and I explained that we were looking for a better hotel and were hoping to see what the rooms were like here. He said: 'Sure.' He told us his name was Stan and we followed him into what appeared to be a suite of 10 or 12 rooms that had its own pantry and kitchen. He invited us to the suite's lounge and offered chips, dip, and sodas. We explained that we were the crew for the new Tajik airline's 747. As we were sitting in the lounge, I finally noticed a big emblem on the wall that read 'U.S. Embassy'. I asked, 'Is this the U. S. Embassy?' 'Yes.' 'Do you work here?' 'Yes.' 'What do you do?' 'I'm the Ambassador.' Stan, the Ambassador, and his charming wife entertained us for the next hour or so as we swapped stories and local intelligence. I asked him about the information I had gotten about local war lords and border positions. He confirmed most of it. The border fighting that was supposedly 150 miles away was now only 80 miles from the city. He explained that he kept a C-130 Hercules airplane on standby 24 hours a day in case it became necessary to evacuate the embassy staff.

(left to right) Earl Speirs, Sherman Carr, and Jim Lank.

U.S. Embassy (hotel)

"That night, the aircraft we were scheduled to fly to Karachi and back overflew Dushanbe because of bad weather. The weather stayed bad and it overflew us again on the way back to London. We were stuck here for another 48 hours. My most immediate concern was to call my wife Mary because she was going to meet me in London. Since I obviously wasn't going to be back in London in time to meet her, I put in the two-hour-to-wait call through Moscow and was relieved when I finally got through and told her to wait two days and come on the next Tajik Air flight out of London. She would then spend one day with me in Dushanbe, and we would continue together to New Delhi, Agra and the Taj Mahal.

"Two things I hadn't counted on happened. The airplane had to overfly one more time and there was a fire fight near our hotel between Russian tanks and rebels with Kalashnikovs and mortars. The rapid fire of modern machine guns is really something. The Russians were using the most modern Gatling gun type that sounded more like an air hose used to clean machine parts except instead of air, it was putting out steel projectiles at a 'zillion' per second. Everything was snow covered so the sounds of the skirmish were eerily muffled. The rebels would fire their Kalashnikovs, and the Russians would answer. I called Mary and told her to stay home."

50

The Last Layover

As the flights continued it was quickly becoming clear that the operation was encountering some severe financial problems and getting the flight successfully off was becoming a day-to-day affair. In addition, there was a mechanical problem with one of the aircraft's engines and it was taken out of service. Eventually *Snow Leopard* was repossessed by United Airlines. Gunilla Crawford and her crew were on the last rotation. They were in Delhi when the aircraft was repossessed.

Gunilla Crawford:

"We arrived in New Delhi on a regular flight and checked in at the Sheraton where we stayed as Pan Am crew. A couple of days later as we are getting ready to take the inbound flight back to London, our Captain informed us that there is a delay. I believe the message read 'buy more beer' or something to that effect.

"We sat by the pool and eventually it became clear that the plane had been impounded and our adventure probably over. It had lasted a little over 4 months. Our Station Manager was stuck with some 500-700 passengers who had booked flights to London. He counted on the crew as pawns for money from London, as we could not leave, and our crew visas would run out. We knew how to quietly go to the authorities and extend the visas without his knowledge. The Station Manager's assistant was helpful. We did not want the hotel to know the dilemma, after all the company was to pay for our rooms. We asked Vince who was in London to fax an explanation to our situation, in Spanish, so the hotel would not find out. They didn't and we got the information we wanted. Time to plan our 'escape'.

The crew waiting in Delhi

51

"The problem was to book a flight, we had to buy the tickets right away and not at the airport when we left. Through a friend in Miami, who was a travel agent and who made a few phone calls, we were booked on Air France to Paris with a connection to London and we were able to pay the morning of the departure. Our Captain footed the bill on his credit card!! An incredible man! On the morning we left we all came down to the lobby, paid our incidentals and went to the airport. We felt an urge to quickly get through security and immigration, and I remember looking around, like the others, to see if the Station Manager would come running to stop us. He didn't, and we were back in London several hours later."

Vince Rossi was in London at the time of the repossession of *Snow Leopard*. He wanted to provide as much information as possible to the Delhi crew without compromising them given the financial situation. He did this by sending information by fax, written in Spanish. In addition, there were Tajik flight attendants laying over in London. They were faced with a different problem.

Vince Rossi:

"The Tajik crew laying over in LHR had purchased MANY frozen chickens to bring home. When it became clear we were not flying that night and it was likely we would not ever fly again, the Tajik flight attendants approached me and expressed concern about the chickens defrosting. It is highly unlikely that the front desk manager from the Sheraton Skyline had ever received the request I was to make. I approached the front desk and asked for a substantial space in the hotel's kitchen freezer to store quite a large number of frozen chickens. The chickens remained there frozen until the Embassy of Tajikistan arranged for transport of the Tajik crews and the frozen chickens back to Dushanbe sometime later."

Gunilla Crawford remained in London for a short while, hoping that the affair was "just a hiccup, and all would be solved in due time." After a few days the sad truth settled in that it was all over and "maybe it had never meant to be more than what it was."

Who would have thought that a remote country in the former Soviet Union would have a Boeing 747 operation linking it with the West? It actually happened - and it could have continued but for fate. The timing was just not perfect for starting such an operation. The infrastructure within Tajikistan's Civil

Aviation Authority had not matured enough to take on the financial and political burden of a complex Sixth Freedom operation, requiring bilateral agreements not only with the United Kingdom, but with India and Pakistan as well. Thanks to the London management, the UK agreement and slots at Heathrow were secured. Unfortunately, the negotiations to secure the agreements with India were still incomplete when the operation started and that presented barriers and resultant revenue losses. Had the start of the operation been delayed until the negotiations were completed there might have been a different result. That will never be known. However, the *Snow Leopard* operation proved that it could be done, and for four short months, *Snow Leopard* proudly flew the skies between London, Dushanbe and Delhi/Karachi.

Made in the USA
Middletown, DE
11 April 2023

28516158R00033